SIGNS

of Our Time

By John Margolies and Emily Gwathmey

ABBEVILLE PRESS • PUBLISHERS • NEW YORK • LONDON • PARIS

Page 1:
Abandoned signs store,
Springfield, Illinois.

Editor: Walton Rawls
Designer: Molly Shields
Production Manager:
Matthew Pimm

Library of Congress
Cataloging-in-Publication Data

Margolies, John.
Signs of our time / by John Margolies and Emily Gwathmey. p. cm.
ISBN 1-55859-209-1
1. United States—Social life and customs—20th century.
2. Advertising, Outdoor—United States—History—20th century.
3. Automobile travel—United States—History—20th century.
I. Gwathmey, Emily Margolin. II. Title.
E169.M324 1993
973—dc20
92-37283
CIP

Contents

Introduction

Not so long ago, to drive the highways and byways of America was a mind-expanding voyage through wonderland. Alongside the road there flashed in staggering profusion an extraordinary assortment of commercial icons. Flying red horses. Soaring eagles. Cheerful bluebirds. Neon flamingos. Colonial church steeples and medieval white towers. Teepee colonies and tourist towns. Simple Simon and a friendly old pieman. A looming dark-green dinosaur. Flashing stars and pointing arrows. Rocket ships and covered wagons. Paul Bunyan and Abe Lincoln. A gigantic Indian maiden and an outsized Southern mammy. Clowns and bellhops and cowboys and chefs. Hamburgers and ice cream cones soaring into the sky. America once was a roadside garden of earthly and exotic delights, a mind-boggling fantasyland of stupendous signs, spectacular statuary, and stunning structures.

Advertising signs glowed and spun and prodded in a dancing display of pyrotechnics. Crafted in all colors of the rainbow, constructed of wood, tin, porcelain enamel, plastic, concrete, neon, or their myriad combinations, signs grabbed imagery from ancient mythology to the atomic

Mammy's Cupboard, Natchez, Mississippi.

◄ **ESSO road map cover, circa 1950s.**

Mobil's Flying Red Horse, Mountain Grove, Missouri.

ENTRANCE

TOURIST TOWN

COURT

UNITED
MOTOR COURT

U. S. Highway 11 & 220–7 Miles North of Roanoke, Va.

Tourist Town, linen postcard circa 1940s.

future. Other signs were ever more literal, relying upon mere letters to spell out choice words, phrases, puns, jokes, or even the entrepreneur's own name. EAT. JOE'S GAS. IT'LL DO MOTEL. Spanning the continent, signs not only throbbed with the pulse of America's creative native spirit but proclaimed the essentials of our free enterprise system. Buy this. Stop here. Consume. Spend.

During the highway heyday, the golden age that stretched from the 1920s on up to World War II, a trip in an automobile was like a gypsy caravan ride through time and space into a landscape of memory populated by remarkable characters who continually presented their come-ons and come-ins to car-happy consumers. These larger-than-life offers of the very best in gas, food, and lodging took on the dazzling graphics and forms of a bold, new commercial folk art. In a frenzy to convince motorists to spend the night *and* their money, highway advertisers turned the roadside into a visually vibrant shopping spree. Early businesses vied madly for the driver's attention. Their imagery, often overlaid with highly regionalized flavors, symbolized the new-found and vitally exciting ambience of life on the open road. Catering to a new form of lust, signs were exuberant, spontaneous, and joyfully individualized, a razzle-dazzle trumpeting of goods and services to a nation on the move.

Roadside artifacts are among the most memorable visual icons of our time. Some of them are entire buildings that actually functioned as signs. Architects Robert Venturi and Denise Scott Brown determined that they were essentially of two types and named them "ducks" and "decorated sheds." "Duck"

◄ Hotel Gibson, matchbook cover.

➤ It'll Do Motel, office, Jonesborough, Tennessee.

➤ **Mother Goose Market, Hazard, Kentucky.**

▼ **Howard Johnson's, Burlington, Vermont.**

comes from the famous Big White Duck structure on Long Island and indicates a building shaped like the product it dispenses. "Decorated shed," on the other hand, is a structure that uses bold, individualized graphic images and colors to help identify the kind of business conducted therein, be it the unmistakable mandarin-red and dragon-bedecked facade of a Main Street Chinese restaurant or the sheltering bright-orange roof of a highway Howard Johnson's. Many of the other great roadside buildings and their symbols tend to be hybrids, part duck, part shed, like the Leaning Tower of Pizza. From Dutch Boy dishing out both paint and ice cream to Pontiac's Indian to Bob's Big Boy, highway artifacts proffer everything from Main Street essentials to off-the-wall tourist distractions.

The Big Duck, Riverhead, N. Y., linen postcard circa 1940s.

Bob's Big Boy, Los Angeles, California.

➤ Golden City Restaurant, Columbus, Ohio.

▼ Bob's, matchbook cover.

America's auto mania came about through several major developments, not the least of which was the discovery of the country's abundant reserves of crude oil. In 1901, the first major "gusher" was drilled at Spindletop Oil Field in Texas. Soon oil companies began refining the crude to get gasoline instead of distilling it for kerosene, since increasing numbers of automobiles needed to get more places faster and cheaper. Then, Henry Ford put out his Model T in 1907 as the "motor car for the great multitude," tapping into a deep reservoir within America's national character, the restless need to keep moving on to new frontiers. With the swift proliferation and widespread availabilty of affordable automobiles, and plenty of gas to keep them going, there sprang up almost instantly a whole new breed of tourists. Eager to free themselves from the rigid constraints of horse-drawn coaches and railroad schedules and to savor the hitherto unimaginable freedom of stopping and going at will, motorists traded in their timetables and trackside hotels for road maps and auto camps.

In 1920 there were eight million automobiles; ten years later, this figure had tripled. From the 1930s on, cars were the principal mode of pleasure traveling. When it was discovered that the glop left over from refining crude oil could be used to improve the roads themselves, the scene was set for traveling in a big way. With a nationwide highway system racing to connect North, South, East, and West, auto-adventurers set out behind the wheel to explore and conquer new frontiers, to "see America first." Just grab the family, hop in the car, and you are an All-American vagabond king of the road.

Mail Pouch Tobacco barn, Riceland, Ohio.

Among the early forms of roadside communication was the commercial message hand-painted on a suitable wall, the most notable of which was the Mail Pouch chewing tobacco advertising sign, painted at first on the train side and then on the highway side of barns. Itinerant sign-painters hired by the tobacco company roamed rural America offering to paint entire barns for free if on one side they could paint CHEW MAIL POUCH—TREAT YOURSELF TO THE BEST. This bold graphic idea evolved into an endless procession of large-scale images set up within convenient view from the road, screaming at drivers to get ready to step on the brakes up ahead. In 1939, in what turned out to be a stroke of promotional genius, the Burma-Shave Company presented alongside the highway their own brand of travel poetry, by means of signs in series, five or six at a time. Such memorable ditties as "HE HAD THE RING/HE HAD THE FLAT/BUT SHE FELT HIS CHIN/AND

Billboard series, Pegram, Tennessee.

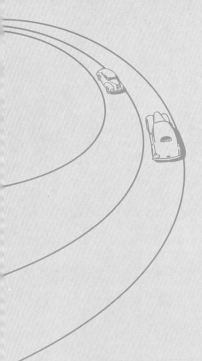

Woolworth, Williston, North Dakota. ➤

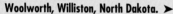

◄ Ahwahnee Motel,
Denver, Colorado.

THAT WAS THAT/BURMA-SHAVE" became an indelible part of the American consciousness.

Sightseeing, shopping, eating, resting, playing—families toured merrily and relentlessly from place to place. They experienced the open landscape and kept an eye on the built environment as it made itself apparent in what would become a typical pattern of urban development: from raw nature to a few houses to a honkytonk strip in no time. The strip had a master plan of its own. Drive-in movies usually marked the very edge of town, because they needed lots of inexpensive real estate and hoped to draw picture-show patrons from neighboring towns. Next came the car dealerships with their huge parking lots, and then the motels with their roadside restaurants. As the strip grew closer to the center of town, its density thickened. However, Main Street had

The Tower Bowl, San Diego, California. ➤

Bildon Ferris Wheel, Hendersonville, North Carolina.

its own agenda, its own set of signs and symbols, smaller, hung lower, and more highly articulated than those found on the strip, since this was where cars moved slower or even halted briefly at stoplights, and people were out of their cars and walking from place to place. Out the other side of town, this procession of commerce and sign art repeated itself in reverse. In the course of a prolonged joyride, one might experience this entire process over and over and over again, as the miles whizzed by.

On Main Street itself, as towns became bigger and bigger, and sign-making became more sophisticated, the simple mortar and pestle for a drugstore or striped pole for a barber shop evolved into signs in some places that were huge multimillion-dollar extravaganzas of color and light. The Great White Way through New York City's Times Square is the most famous and flashiest example, a perpetual psychedelic light show created long before anyone ever heard of hippie culture. The signs themselves in Times Square became a major tourist attraction, and people would come by subway, cab, or on foot to stare in wonder. In downtown Dallas, the flying red horse displayed at many a roadside gas station became an enormous Pegasus, forty feet wide by thirty-two feet high, soaring 450 feet in the air above a twenty-nine-story office building, visible from miles away.

Years ago, it was popular to "go for a ride," to drive randomly along the blacktops and in and out of neighboring towns. Perhaps it was just for the newfound pleasure of being on the move or for the joy of discovering odd new establishments and quirky signs in

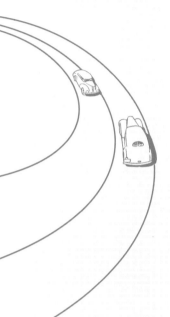

Times Square at Night, New York City, linen postcard circa 1940s.

McDonald's, Downey, California.

Buster Brown Shoes, Jacksonville, Florida.

unknown territory. Maybe there would be a new ethnic restaurant with a quaint Buddha image at curbside, or an exotic snake farm, or a root beer barrel building, or a gas station dispensing gasoline from within an iceberg. The highways of America in the first half of the twentieth century beckoned a new breed of auto-adventurer into a commercial phantasmagoria beyond his wildest dreams.

This brave and bold new advertising medium was spawned by pioneering mom-and-pop entrepreneurs offering up seductive goods and services to be viewed first by the passing automotive parade through freshly polished windshields. They developed their own highly individualistic, varied imagery, and the highway habitat grew quickly into a delirious realm that offered consumption as a potent form of entertainment. At every bend of the road, a new experience or opportunity awaited. STOP HERE, screamed sign after sign. Driver and passengers were jolted to attention on their way

◄ Uncle Sam Fast Food, Toledo, Ohio.

Snake Farm, La Place, Louisiana.

Joy Theatre,
San Antonio, Texas.

➤ Moby Dick Motel, Route 6, Dartmouth, Massachusetts.

ANIMATED ELECTRIC SIGN (Easter Scene)

JUNGE'S

AT THE HOME OF **JUNGE'S BAKERY PRODUCTS** · JOPLIN, MO.

OB-HS59

Junge's Bakery Products, Joplin, Missouri, linen postcard circa 1940s.

through the Grand Roadside Department Store of the U.S.A.

So-called "progress" marked the beginning of the end of this great tradition of American graphic art and design, as faceless corporate logos, 800 numbers, and television commercials were in the ascendency at the expense of quirky individuality. The interstate highway system, with its uniform 55 and 65 mph speed limits and no unfranchised roadside businesses allowed, bypassed the old major highways, turning them into untraveled byways. And then the Highway Beautification Act of 1965 banished most signs and billboards into the deep background of America's driving experience. Anacronistic main streets and old downtowns were replaced by shopping malls set on the outskirts of town. Invented to serve the new suburban developments beyond the strips, the malls generally displayed no obtrusive signs beyond the name of the shopping center itself.

Huge conglomerates replaced small family businesses nationwide with franchised look-alikes. Drive-in restaurants became McDonald's and their ilk. Small neighborhood gas stations gave way to the large supermarket types that dispensed only gas and oil—no checking the oil or wiping the windshield. Cozy Camps were gradually transformed into motel chains of identical accommodations. In 1953 the Holiday Inn empire was born when Kemmon Wilson opened his first motor court on a strip outside of Memphis, Tennessee. The

➤ Westland Service, Drake, North Dakota.

Oldsmobile Service, Smith Center, Kansas.

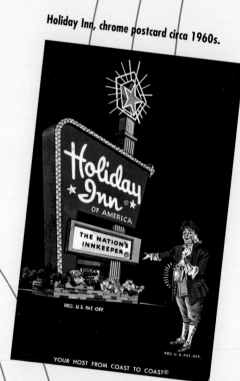

Holiday Inn, chrome postcard circa 1960s.

◄ Borden's,
Longview, Texas.

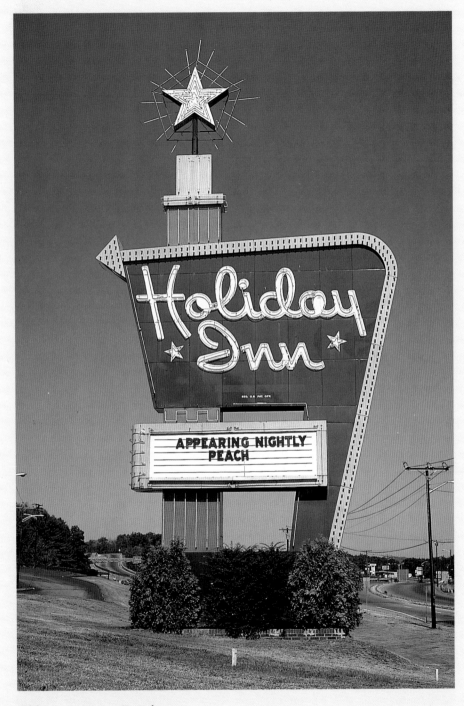

Holiday Inn, Leominster, Massachusetts.

original Holiday Inn sign was part of the old iconic tradition, an orgy of neon and lightbulbs and arrows modeled after a movie marquee blinking green, yellow, orange, pink, blue, red, and white. In the mid 1950s, a friendly colonial guy named Johnny Holiday was added to the act. However, by the 1980s, all of this had become too folksy and was replaced by a bland, dark-green sign, with only the name Holiday Inn visible in white, inner-lit plastic letters.

Sadly, what happened to Holiday Inn was symptomatic of what happened to the personality of many other businesses across the land. Homogenization and its inevitable blandness were now the new rule of commerce. With geographical distinctions and individuality erased, a strip outside of Denver would be interchangeable with a strip on the outskirts of Boston—or any place else, for that matter. Idiosyncratic symbols full of humor and life degraded into corporate abstractions, mirroring the inevitable transformation of driving from a fascinating adventure into a time-consuming, boring chore. Getting there used to be at least half the fun; now it's practically no fun at all.

Friend O' Mine:
Drive slowly and avoid accidents.
We appreciate your patronage and ask for a continuance of same.
Sincerely,
Mister Slippery

➤ Octopus Car Wash, Minneapolis, Minnesota.

▼ Light House Tavern, old Highway 2, Wenatchee, Washington.

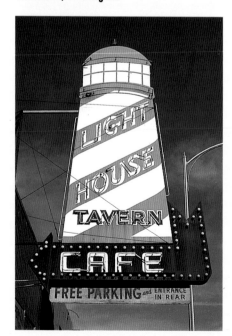

Transportation

St. Joseph Auto and Furniture Fabric, St. Joseph, Missouri.

➤ **Vince Kolb Auto Sales, Jefferson City, Missouri.**

*E*ver since the arrival of Christopher Columbus, the common denominator in the history of America has been the idea of exploration and movement toward new frontiers. Therefore, it is not surprising that transportation imagery and the movement it implies have been used to create some of the most striking advertising signs and symbols of the twentieth century. The act of getting there has often been as compelling as "there" itself, whether one went by covered wagon, boat, train, plane, car, or even by rocket ship or flying saucer.

Transportation suggests adventure, even if it's just a trip around the block. The automobile, that mainstay of personal mobility, inspired an incredible array of signs. Very often the automobile itself is the sign, lifted away from its asphalt context to a rooftop, or suspended from horizontal supports. Jalopies right out of a 1940s gangster movie ride high in the sky to proclaim used-car opportunities, drive-in restaurants, or a nightclub featuring doo wop music from the golden age of rock 'n' roll. Gasoline, that vital fluid, is tied to mythic and even extraterrestrial symbols, as well as to more down-to-earth exemplars like Pegasus, dinosaurs, scallop shells, and sputnik. The face of a comical local gas-station attendant in Montana beams contentedly from beneath the visor of his uniform cap as the cars come and go.

Arks, galleons, and sailboats glide atop macadam seas, with neon lighthouses guiding the way. In New Jersey, a ship-shaped building patterned after the Santa Maria was originally used as a lure for a real estate development company, while Ark Fast Food in North Carolina drew its symbolism from Biblical times. The roadside armada could boast ships of every sort.

Huffing and puffing along imaginary tracks, locomotives signified restaurants, motels, and gift shops. Flying in air or grounded, planes and bombs and rocket ships called attention to gas stations, bars, and roller-skating rinks.

The fleet of transporation artifacts alongside the American highway urged travelers on the move to continue seeking new frontiers.

Town Gate, Wareham, Massachusetts.

Atomic Bar, El Paso, Texas.

Santa Maria Building, Absecon, New Jersey.

1941 Cafe, Lowell, Arkansas.

➤ Mel-Haven Lodge, Colorado Springs, Colorado.

▲ LR Used Cars, Hendersonville, North Carolina.

▲ Ritter Auto Parts, Monroe, Louisiana.

▲ Razorback Auto Sales, Fayetteville, Arkansas.

▲ Dependable Used Cars, Grand Rapids, Michigan.

◄ Eddie Clark's Used Cars, Montpelier, Vermont.

W hat better way to advertise a used-car lot than to show a great used car? The driver of the blue 1950s classic even waves his arm as an added come on. When these signs were built, some of those airborne vehicles were just that—not the classic relics they are now. Although Vermont banished commercial signs years earlier, Eddie Clark's used-car sign, with its prominent tail fins, remained as one of the last highway survivors in the state.

▼ Ruby Falls, Chattanooga, Tennessee.

1934 SINCLAIR ROAD MAP

SINCLAIR
OHIO

▲ Yale trucking company, New York, New York, postcard.

◀ Blue Bird Truck Stop, Atlanta, Georgia.

By the late 1920s, service station owners had learned they could make lots more money if, besides gasoline and oil, they sold TBAs—industry jargon for tires, batteries, and accessories. Soon specialty shops evolved for nearly every aspect of automotive service. In 1962, in Philadelphia, Earl Scheib promised to "paint any car any color" for $19.95. The idea caught on, and the Scheib Empire spread from coast to coast. Now it costs $129.95! This early California version of Earl's sign includes a globe encircled in neon by vintage coupes, recalling the good old days when painting a car was still a bargain. Stan the Tire Man just sells tires, but out front he had a 1960s-style Tire Woman who seemed to be a close relative of Jackie Kennedy.

Stan the Tire Man, Mount Vernon, Illinois.

Indian Gas, Lawrence, Kansas.

▲ Earl Scheib,
Beverly Hills, California.

➤ Razorback Gas, Siloam Springs, Arkansas.

In 1936, Harry Kalbach's father commissioned from the Nebraska Neon Sign Company in Lincoln an image of a service station attendant in a blue uniform and peaked cap. The sign has stood ever since in Menlo, Iowa, on old Highway 6 (now bypassed by the new Interstate), its mechanical arm having beckoned to passing motorists for three generations. In its salad days, the entire sign, including the arm, was outlined in neon. For a while the arm no longer moved, but Harry had it repaired, and it now creaks as it waves to the nearly nonexistant passing parade.

◄ Kalbach Oil, Menlo, Iowa.

◄ Space Station Gas, Craig, Colorado.

▼ Dunham's Gas, Billings, Montana.

▼ Jet Gas, Mathison, Mississippi.

➤ Richfield Gas, Ely, Nevada.

➤ Covered Wagon Bar,
Bismarck, North Dakota.

Sioux Chief Train Motel, Sioux Falls, South Dakota.

➤ Loose Caboose Gift Shop, Whitefish, Montana.

The Loose Caboose is not a caboose, but a small building with a skylight next to a real caboose in rural Montana. A caboose was also used at Motel 36 in Texas, although not as its sign—it was the lounge and snack bar for a group of motel rooms concocted from side-tracked freight cars. The sign, an image of an old locomotive, completed the freight-train motif. Verl Thomson's Sioux Chief Train Motel is much more direct and to the point, with sleeping cars lined up beside the road on tracks.

Motel 36, Somerville, Texas.

◄ French's Lionel Train House, Des Moines, Washington.

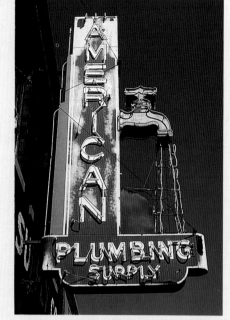

▲ American Plumbing Supply, Des Moines, Iowa.

▼ Bob's Shoe Repair, Rapid City, South Dakota.

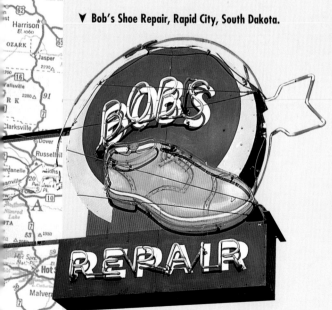

Pete's Cafe, Boonville, Missouri, linen postcard circa 1940s.

PETE'S AIR-CONDITIONED CAFE

314 MAIN STREET   BOONVILLE, MISSOURI

Main Street

Theater row, Dallas, Texas, linen postcard.

Mendes Park Western Wear, Fresno, California.

Downtown U.S.A. was America's earliest urban marketplace, where people gathered together in a central location to peddle their wares. The trade signs they used were smaller than those out on the open road, and they were hung close to street level, to entice the customers who came by on foot, in horse-drawn buggies, or, later, in automobiles to stop and shop in the commercial district of town.

Main Street provided services that would take consumers from cradle to grave, and signs for life's basic necessities often beckoned in literal forms. There were plumbing supply faucets dripping neon water, hats and shoes in a splendid array of shapes and sizes, and keys and hammers indicating locksmith shops and hardware stores. When it came to banks and funeral parlors, the signage was more digni-fied, projecting a formal and institutional aura to assure and reassure their customers.

Some merchants based their signs upon ancient and abstract symbols, like the pawn-broker's three golden balls, the cigar store's Indian, and the barber's pole. The barber's symbol goes back to medieval times when the local barber also practiced minor surgery and bloodletting—a popular treatment for numer-ous ailments. Before the patient's vein was

Mayflower Cafe, Cheyenne, Wyoming, linen postcard circa 1940s.

VFW and Boy Scout Building, Cheyenne, Wyoming.

Hartstone Flower Shop,
Weymouth, Massachusetts.

FLOWERS

Gamberi's Shoe Service, Natchez, Mississippi.

opened, he steadied his arm by grasping the barber's pole, which regularly was stained by streams of blood that spiraled down it. The red-and-white barber pole evolved as an abstraction of this.

As America's oldest shopping center, Main Street had a lighter side as well, for many businesses catered less to essential and more to enjoyable pursuits. The snazziest buildings in town were movie theaters because they sold entertainment rather than essentials. Jewelry shops showed perfectly cut diamonds to characterize their wares, while a midwestern fur salon let a friendly white polar bear announce its repair and remodeling services.

Whether it was the ubiquitous golden Woolworth "W" or a highly individualized sign artfully crafted by local artisans that caught your eye, your trip along Main Street was a journey back into a time when small businesses created their own remarkable and highly idiosyncratic iconography.

Doc & Elmer Key Service, St. Louis, Missouri.

Broadway Style House, Shreveport, Louisiana.

➤ South-Chester Drive-In,
Bakersfield,
California,
matchbook cover.

▲ Centre Theater,
Salt Lake City, Utah,
matchbook cover.

◀ Strand Theater, Shreveport, Louisiana.

Alder Theatre, Portland, Oregon, postcard circa 1930.

ALDER STREET, PORTLAND, OREGON

FROZEN JUSTICE TALKING

COLUMBIA COMMERCIAL STUDIOS, INC.

◄ Reel Joy Theater,
King City, California.

The most ornate and whimsical of all downtown buildings were the movie theaters, whose signs went so far as to proclaim their diverting purpose: there was a Pastime in Danville, Arkansas, an Amusu in Corpus Christi, Texas, and there still is Reel Joy to be had in rural central California. A more sophisticated idea—that of elegance and glitz—is conveyed by the Strand Theater's very name. Its sign, with an orgy of tracer bulbs and neon exploding into a red-and-yellow crown, adorns one of the snazziest theaters in all of Louisiana.

REEL JOY

ANOTHER U

While some people were content with passive relaxation at the movies, others went for more interactive recreation. The thrills and spills of the roller rink were excitingly conveyed on a sign in Oklahoma: a winged skate atop a 1950s rocket. In Tucson, a neon bowling lanes sign promises a strike every time, as a ball repeatedly smashes into ten pins.

At these recreational establishments, the most popular pastime of them all is always right at hand, be it a shot of rye, a glass of beer, or both—in that order and in rapid succession.

Moose Club, Rochester, New York, linen postcard circa 1950.

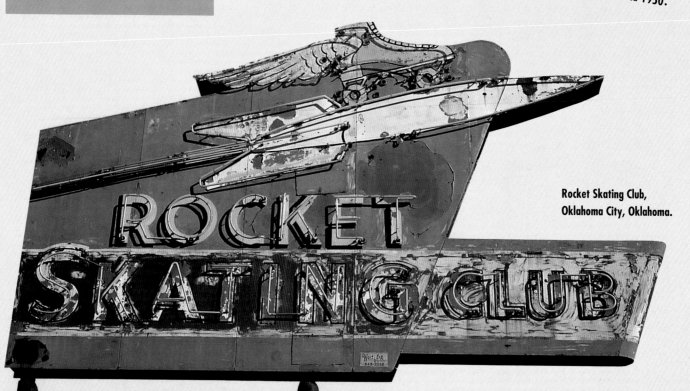

Rocket Skating Club, Oklahoma City, Oklahoma.

◄ Loyal Order of Moose, Billings, Montana.

➤ Keglers Lanes,
Tucson, Arizona.

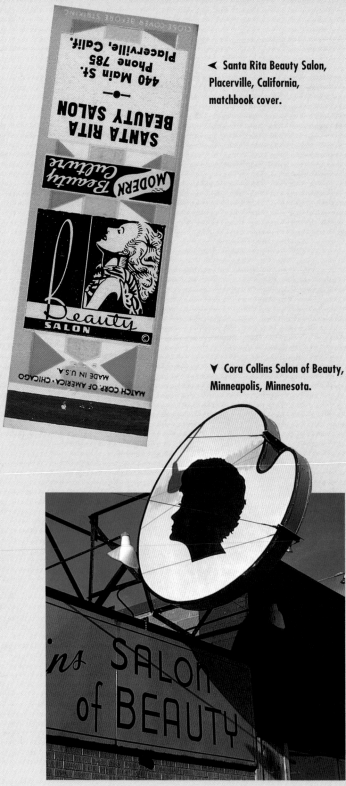

◄ Santa Rita Beauty Salon,
Placerville, California,
matchbook cover.

CLOSE COVER BEFORE STRIKING

440 Main St.
Phone 785
Placerville, Calif.

SANTA RITA
BEAUTY SALON

MODERN Beauty Culture

beauty
SALON

MATCH CORP. OF AMERICA · CHICAGO
MADE IN U.S.A.

▼ Cora Collins Salon of Beauty,
Minneapolis, Minnesota.

▲ Burt's Barber Shop,
Seattle, Washington.

FONDREN
BEAUTY Inc.
SALON
SCHOOL

ins SALON
of BEAUTY

◄ Fondren Beauty Salon,
Jackson, Mississippi.

Barber poles have come in many sizes, shapes, and configurations—in addition to the familiar street poles at curbside and the hypnotically swirling signs attached to buildings. In northern Louisiana, an old industrial tank was pressed into service, while at Burt's in Seattle the pole has been flattened into an abstraction.

The symbol for beauty parlors is less universal, the usual formula being the beautician's name and the words "Beauty Shop." But at Cora's the artistry is more expressive: a palette-shaped, inner-lit plastic sign displays a beautifully coiffed black silhouette in dramatic contrast to its shocking-pink background.

◄ **North Side Barber Shop, Monroe, Louisiana.**

► **Longoria Barber Shop, Harlingen, Texas.**

43963

Freestanding street clocks have nearly disappeared from today's urban streetscape, but other clocks remain an important element in signs for a variety of businesses. Along with the obligatory diamond drawing, a real clock was particularly appropriate for a jewelry store sign—to remind consumers of the pocket and wrist varieties available within.

An especially elaborate neon sign for a jewelry shop in Utah used the clock as the center for a beautiful white flower with extensive green tendrils. But its time was up long ago, and the site on Ogden's Main Street is now a verdant patch of lawn.

◄ Washington Street, Boston, Massachusetts, linen postcard circa 1940.

Smalley's Jewelry, Ogden, Utah.

Wimmer's Jewelry, Fargo, North Dakota.

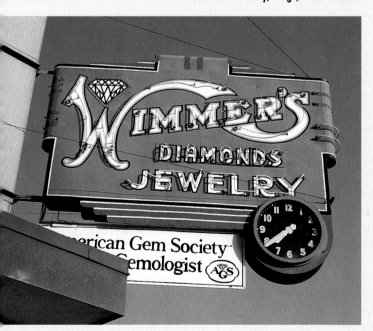

➤ Dana Bushong Jewelry, Ft. Madison, Iowa.

*C*reatures great and small have always been a popular way to advertise a product or a business—either literally or symbolically. Mobil's Flying Red Horse is the definitive mythic example. The greyhound's marriage to a bus company is another inductive leap. At full stride, this noble canine conveys a speedy trip on a long-distance bus, an idea definitely predating the jet plane.

Other signs are much more direct and literal. The great white bear depicted at a fur repair shop is the very stuff a damaged coat might be made of, while a sign at a local aquarium in Alabama depicts the proper angel fish for the tank in a 1950s living room.

◄ Zenthoefer Furs, St. Louis, Missouri.

Woodcraft Hobby Store, Minneapolis, Minnesota.

ALAQUATICS Tropical Fish, Birmingham, Alabama.

▼ Greyhound Bus Depot,
Salinas, California.

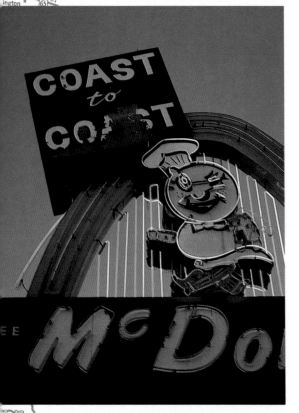

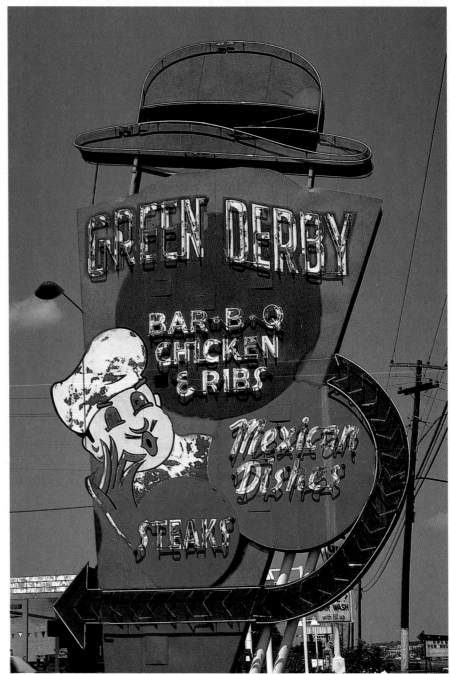

▲ Speedee the McDonald's Chef, Azusa, California.

◄ Leaning Tower of Pizza, Quincy, Massachusetts.

Food & Drink

Roadside food is all about being quick. Merchants resort to a kind of shorthand to project the very essence of the culinary experiences they offer. The food itself is prototypical short-order American fare—tempting treats a ten-year-old would love to eat every day for every meal, forever. Hot dogs. Hamburgers. French fries. Soft drinks. Ice cream. And for the road-weary grownup, there's the invigorating and ubiquitous cup of java. In the mountains of New Mexico one spot actually promises a cup of "200-mile coffee."

Since everybody stops to eat, what could be more inviting on a sign than a happy chef, reassuring hungry travelers of clean, well-prepared, and wholesome road food. Roadside chefs baked cakes, told time, and barbecued at eateries across the land. Of them all, the most familiar American chef is Howard Johnson's Pieman, who has tempted Simple Simon with his wares since the early 1930s. When the McDonald brothers started selling fast food, they too employed chef imagery. Long before Ronald McDonald came to represent the company, a hamburger-headed man called Speedee cooked burgers and fries atop parabolic golden arches.

▲ Howard Johnson's, matchbook cover.

➤ Happy Chef, Cherokee, Iowa.

Round Up Lounge, Highway 30, Fargo, North Dakota.

One of the most popular ways to make the traveler stop for a bit to eat is to construct a building or sign that is an oversized replica of the comestible itself, or at least the container it comes in. The Tail o' the Pup in Los Angeles is a giant hot dog with mustard, the mid section of which hinges up to form an awning over the food counter. Built in the 1930s and now the last survivor of a series of frankfurter stands, this building achieved landmark status from turning up in countless movies, television shows, and commercials. Not nearly so well known but every bit as spectacular is the Coney Island Dairyland hot dog building, located southeast of Denver, with cascades of mustard and mountains of relish oozing off each end of the dog sticking out beyond the concrete roll.

Not all "ducks" serve what they portray. The Teapot, built in 1933 in Chester, West Virginia, dishes out hot dogs as well as souvenirs—but little tea. The Teapot Dome building in Zillah, Washington, inspired by the famous scandal of Warren G. Harding's administration, has been dispensing petroleum to cars for nearly seventy years. And the California Root Beer Barrel drive-in survives today as an unlikely home for the Rice Bowl Chinese Restaurant.

One can certainly assume that ice cream is the most popular road food of them all.

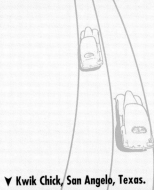

> Bar 17 Club, Billings, Montana.

▼ Kwik Chick, San Angelo, Texas.

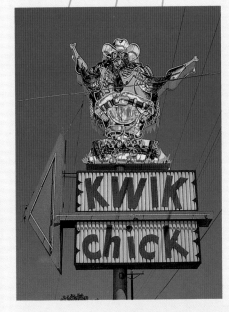

▲ Christie's Restaurant, Houston, Texas.

> Spur Bar, Billings, Montana.

Sisson's Coffee Pot, Port Malobar, Florida, linen postcard.

SISSON'S COFFEE POT — ON THE BEAUTIFUL INDIAN RIVER

▼ Coney Island Dairy Land, Aspen Park, Colorado.

▼ Tail o'the Pup, Los Angeles, California.

▲ Knapp's Good Food, Garbersville, California, pamphlet.

➤ The Kegs, Grand Forks, North Dakota.

Teapot Dome Service Station, Zillah, Washington, 1922 (National Register of Historic Places).

Nearly every town of any size has an ice cream sign, sometimes derived from arctic and Eskimo themes, like igloos and icebergs. But more often, signs take the form of a soft-serve cone with a meltingly inviting curlicue tip. The names of these establishments are short and catchy. There are Dairy Kings, Dairy Queens, Zesto, Besto, Little Dippers, Oliver Twists, and even Dairy Dreams.

Many purveyors of culinary delights push their products through incongruous associations. Chinese restaurants project visions of chop suey and egg rolls by enlisting images of Buddhas, pagodas, and dragons. The Leaning Tower of Pisa becomes the Leaning Tower of Pizza. But beer barrels and stoneware steins hark back to Oktoberfests in Munich and the bierstubes of old Heidelberg.

Deep in the heart of Texas are two particularly remarkable cowboy variants: a three-dimensional shrimp sculpture in Houston that wears a ten-gallon hat and aims his six-guns at the roadway, and a neoned cowboy-chicken at the Kwik Chick in San Angelo that packs drumsticks in his holsters instead of firearms.

Not to be outdone, cowgirls got into the sign business as well. An appropriately attired cowgirl swings a lasso above her head at the Round Up Lounge in North Dakota, while a sublimely happy party gal languishes in a martini glass, neon boots pointing the way to good food and good times at a bar in Montana.

Experiencing roadside food signs is a visual treat. Tempting buildings encrusted with neon confections are every bit as esthetically delicious as the food is gratifying.

▼ Pancake Place, Tulsa, Oklahoma.

▼ Donut Hole, La Puente, California.

Eel River Cafe, Garberville, California.

The Donut Hole outside Los Angeles, two huge donuts on each end of a drive-through shed, is a perfect example of the "duck," a building type that functions both as a sign and a clue to the products for sale within. A friendly attendant will pass a delicious bagful through your car window for mile after mile of instant snack-gratification. However, a sit-down breakfast is well-nigh irresistible for hungry drivers who come upon the tantalizing light show of oozing neon syrup along old Route 66 or the acrobatic chef flipping perfect neon flapjacks on the old Redwood Highway.

➤ **Navajo Hogan, Colorado Springs, Colorado.**

The Fish Inn was built in the early 1920s. Even expert fisherman have trouble determining its precise piscatorial identity. It most closely resembles a large-mouthed bass—in fact the mouth serves as the entryway to the building, which is sheathed in shiny scalelike shingles. A 1930s real-photo postcard with a view from the hill behind reveals the fish's strategic location by the side of old Highway 10, and directly in front of a string of tourist cabins. The world's largest tiger muskie also has a big mouth, but it doesn't lead anywhere.

▲ Fish Inn, Coeur D'Alene, Idaho, circa 1980s.

➤ Fish Inn, photo postcard circa 1930s.

33737 - FISH INN near Coeur d'Alene

Tiger Muskie, Nevis, Minnesota, linen postcard circa 1950.

World's Largest Tiger Muskie

Located in Nevis, Minnesota

1C-H69

▼ Yoken's Restaurant,
Portsmouth,
New Hampshire.

THAR SHE BLOWS!
YOKEN'S
GOOD THINGS TO EAT

OPEN

▼ Valley View Lodge, Chittenango, New York.

▼ Original Pig Stand, San Antonio, Texas.

➤ Kream Kastle, Brownsville, Tennessee.

➤ Pussy Cat Lounge, Fargo, North Dakota.

➤ Golden Pheasant Restaurant, Sunnyside, Washington.

◄ Shanghai Cafe, Centralia, Washington.

In the culinary garden of roadside America, all pigs great and small have everything to do with barbecues. In San Antonio, Texas, the great Original Pig Stand building, with flashing lightbulbs for eyes, began its life predictably, serving pork sandwiches. It was moved and went on to become a ladies restroom outside a night spot, and, lately, it has turned into a deserted and decaying old shed. Beef on the hoof rarely stands for "Seafood"—except, perhaps, in Chittenango.

D.88. HALIFAX CREAMERY INC., "THE HOME OF SAFE MILK", DAYTONA BEACH, FLA.

PURE MILK

116078

Hallifax Creamery Milk Bottle Dairy, Daytona Beach, Florida, postcard.

YOU'LL Enjoy

AUBREY'S

DAIRY FREEZE

SLUSHES   SUNDAES
BURGERS & SHAKES

CHICKEN BASKET
FISH STICKS
SHRIMP BASKET
BAR·B·QUE

▲ **Aubrey's Dairy Freeze, old Route 66, Shamrock, Texas.**

Maine is one of a growing number of states that strictly regulate roadside signs for commercial buildings. All must be small and tasteful. Nonetheless, an Incredible Hulktype with an enormous hand-dipped ice cream cone looms large atop the Kelbees' Ice Cream Stand. Soft ice cream is a much easier sell beside the road, because the magic twirl at the top of the cone results in a neon signmaker's dream.

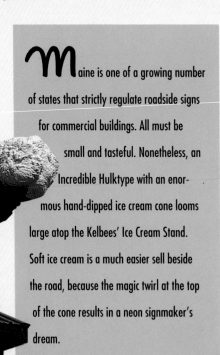

Rummel's ICE CREAM

◄ **Kelbees' Ice Cream Stand, East Winthrop, Maine.**

Snowtop Ice Cream, Livingston, Louisiana.

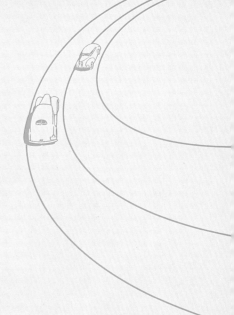

▼ Freezo Ice Cream,
Knoxville, Tennessee.

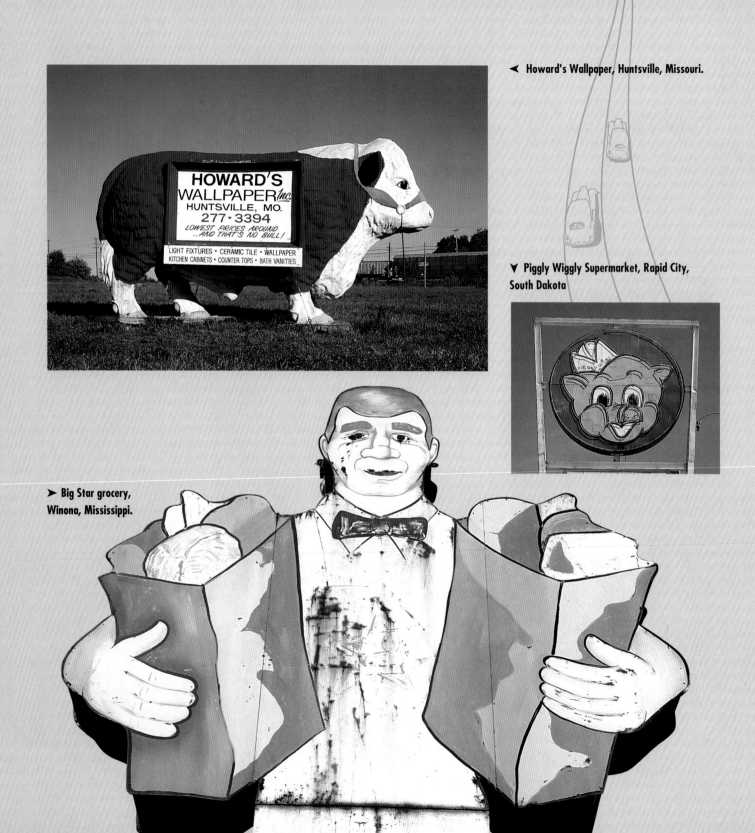

◄ Howard's Wallpaper, Huntsville, Missouri.

HOWARD'S WALLPAPER *Inc.*
HUNTSVILLE, MO.
277·3394
LOWEST PRICES AROUND
...AND THAT'S NO BULL!
LIGHT FIXTURES • CERAMIC TILE • WALLPAPER
KITCHEN CABINETS • COUNTER TOPS • BATH VANITIES

▼ Piggly Wiggly Supermarket, Rapid City,
South Dakota

➤ Big Star grocery,
Winona, Mississippi.

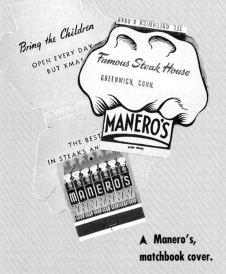

▲ Manero's,
matchbook cover.

While most edible animals will
go straight to the slaughterhouse, full of
promising flavors and loads of cholesterol, it
seems that old steakhouse bull statues will
never die. They don't even fade away. At
least not in the case of this brightly painted
bovine apotheosis, now oddly recycled to
shill the merits ("and that's no bull!") of
Howard's Wallpaper, a home-decorating
center in the Midwest. The smiling neon
Piggly Wiggly porker and Pete's cameo cow,
floating majestically above an arrow of
tracer bulbs, logically signify markets that
sell meat off the hoof, be it a center-cut
pork chop or a T-bone steak.

▲ Pete's Meat Market, El Paso, Texas.

▼ Wall Drug, Wall, South Dakota.

HEAR COWBOY ORCHESTRA
LIFE SIZE · ANIMATED
WALL DRUG

▲ South of the Border, Dillon, South Carolina.

Storybook Land Park, Aberdeen, South Dakota.

Roadside Attractions

Hogan Indian Arts & Crafts Shop, Mancos, Colorado.

➤ Castle Rock,
St. Ignace, Michigan.

To benefit from the boredom of a cross-country trip, crafty entrepreneurs have set up a hodgepodge of unnecessary but totally beguiling excuses to stop, stretch, spend a few bucks, and look at whatever there is before pressing onward. Roadside attractions usually announce themselves through serial signs many miles in advance, increasing their frequency and intensity as the great spots loom closer. The more famous the tourist attraction the more signs there are.

Rock City, atop Lookout Mountain near Chattanooga, Tennessee, is a scenic overlook where, on a clear day, one can view seven states. It's heralded from Maine to Florida by a nearly infinite number of birdhouses and painted barns screaming SEE ROCK CITY. The signs don't tell what it is or where it is. Seemingly, the tourist learns that by homing in as the signs grow in number and frequency.

The Wall Drug Store began life as a tiny pharmacy in Wall, South Dakota, in the early 1930s. Sixty years later, it has become a multimillion-dollar nirvana of insane delights. An attendance record was set one day in July 1989 when more than 22,000 sightseers crossed the threshold.

In the early days, owners Ted and Dorothy Hustead first put up their now-famous

◄ Monkey Island, Hollywood, California, matchbook cover.

◄ "Chatty Belle," gift shop statue, Neilsville, Wisconsin.

▼ Rock City Birdhouse, Ringgold, Georgia.

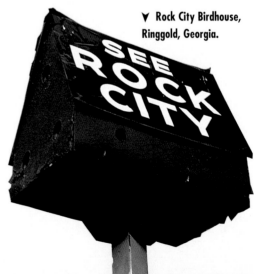

sign just outside of town and promised "free ice water." The signs and the tourists have been proliferating ever since. The Husteads maintain approximately 245 signs, scattered for hundreds of miles in every direction. But to those who have seen them on the road, it must seem that there are many, many more. Additional untold thousands of replica signs are given away each year, and the Husteds will even make up custom signs. One order came from the Casa Botin restaurant (mentioned in Hemingway's *The Sun Also Rises*) and resulted in the outrageous message that Madrid is only 6,223 miles away from Wall Drug.

Wall Drug signs promote one or another outlandish aspect of this drugstore gone amuck—including the Back Yard with its playground and Mt. Rushmore replica; Sam, the piano-playing gorilla; and the Cowboy Orchestra, a coin-operated cornball quartet. The signs come to a climax at the interstate exit, where an enormous fifty-ton brontosaurus screams at the tourist that THIS IS THE PLACE. Just past the dinosaur, one final message reminds those resisting the previous hundreds that "You are missing Wall Drug."

Today, automobiles themselves have become traveling billboards, and even on New York City's Upper West Side, one can come across a van bearing the bumper sticker "Have you dug Wall Drug?" That's total saturation.

Beyond Wall Drug and Rock City, the scope and range of America's wacky leisure-time landscape boggles the mind. There are snake farms, caves, enchanted forests, fairylands, petting zoos, the Thing?, Santa's workshops, and mystery spots, to name just a few. Life on the road would be boring indeed without these opportunities for whimsical fun and games.

DC-214—Three Beauties in Parrot Jungle, Miami, Fla.

Three Beauties, Parrot Jungle, linen postcard circa 1940s.

▲ Entrance, Parrot Jungle, Miami, Florida.

Linen postcard circa 1940s.

Miami's Parrot Jungle is certainly one of the most beautiful and beguiling roadside attractions anywhere. Along its meandering paths, myriad creatures reveal themselves amidst the lush tropical foliage. The climax of this tourist safari is a performing bird show where a parrot pushes a wheelbarrow, and a crested cockatoo makes a trip to the moon and back.

The final stop, just before the gift shop, is the "photo opportunity" area, where a multitude of macaws adorn a visitor's shoulders and arms while a friendly photographer captures this magical experience forever.

▲ Tyranosaurus Rex welcome statue, Vernal, Utah.

➤ Thunderbeast Park, Chiloquin, Oregon.

Gatorland, Route 1, St. Augustine, Florida.

Petrified Wood Park, Lemmon, South Dakota.

LEMMON'S PETRIFIED WOOD PARK

Gatorland

ALLIGATORS !!! 6 MILES

· GIFT SHOP · · COVERED WALKWAYS ·

Gatorland Zoo, Christmas, Florida.

Everglades Safari, Route 41, Dade County, Florida.

Anyone who has ever visited an alligator farm knows that these reptiles just lie there torpidly in the water, never making a move. Nonetheless, they hold a certain primeval fascination. Any action happens at the scheduled demonstrations, where a whole lot of wrestling and snapping goes on. Swampy the Giant, built in 1989 on the old road to Orlando, keeps alive the tradition of outrageous alligator signs. This reptile is longer than a twenty-story building, with a gift shop in its head. The rest of Swampy is a fence that blocks a view of the swampy mire located behind it.

In one tall tale after another, Paul Bunyan, giant woodsman of the American frontier, embodies the strength and ingenuity of lumbermen in the great Northwest. His statue at the entrance to the Trees of Mystery attraction on the coast of Northern California may be the tallest Paul of them all. His boots alone are ten feet high, and an enormous baby-blue Babe looms at his left side. The most artful statues of Paul and Babe were a WPA project in the 1930s, and they still stand proudly in Bemidji, Minnesota, as a major draw for tourists.

▲ Moqui Indian Trading Post, Route 40, Roosevelt, Utah.

➤ Yei-Be-Chi Dancer sign, Indian Gift Shop, Williams, Arizona.

Paul Bunyan and Babe, Trees of Mystery,
Redwood Highway, Klamath, California.

BM-17—Paul Bunyan and Babe, his Blue Ox

OB-H662

Paul Bunyan and Babe, Bemidji, Minnesota, linen postcard circa 1940.

PAUL BUNYAN

LUMBERJACK
MEALS

ALL YOU
CAN EAT OPEN 7 AM

OPEN

FREE
TICKETS
FREE
GAS

◄ Paul Bunyan
Lumberjack Meals,
Wisconsin Dells, Wisconsin.

Conneaut Lake Park, Pennsylvania, linen postcard circa 1950s.

MINIATURE GOLF

Miniature Golf Course
Conneaut Lake Park, Pa.

Indiana Beach, Shafer Lake, Indiana, linen postcard circa 1950s.

Miniature Golf, Beach and Pier seen from Roof Garden—Boardwalk in Foreground

Indiana Beach, Shafer Lake

▼ Photograph, circa 1932,
Litchfield, Illinois.

Miniature golf has been charming and seducing afficionados since its invention in the late 1920s at Rock City, near Chattanooga, Tennessee. Popularity surged after World War II, and again in the 1980s. Dutch McGrath, a present-day miniature golf entrepreneur, has built dozens of Sir Goony Golf courses throughout the United States. The centerpiece of his flagship operation in Chattanooga is a retired tire man statue who has taken up a putter in Dutch's garden of windmills, lighthouses, and bizarre flora and fauna.

◄ ▼ Sir Goony Golf Course, Chattanooga, Tennessee.

Restaurant, Flintstone's Bedrock City, Valle, Arizona.

Television comes to life at Flintstone's Bedrock City. Like most roadside attractions, what's going on inside is hidden by a tall fence, but at the edge of the road, painted on rocks, are promises of rest rooms and tee shirts. Pay to get behind the fence and discover a rather disappointing bunch of small-scale buildings and statues of Wilma, Barney, and the rest of the gang. Although the TV cartoon show is more compelling, this is, nonetheless, a pleasant place to relax and make the kids happy as the long drive continues.

Rest Rooms Rock, Bedrock City.

Entrance, Bedrock City.

Parking lot dinosaur, Bedrock City.

▼ Caveman bench, Dinosaur Gardens, Ossineke, Michigan

➤ Cleveland Lloyd Dinosaur Quarry, Huntington, Utah.

Photo opportunity statue, Marineland, near St. Augustine, Florida.

"Waltz Time", Diver and Model, Marine Studios

Waltz Time, Marineland, Florida, linen postcard circa 1940s.

Entrance arch, Marineland Florida.

arineland, a fish and sea mammal attraction south of St. Augustine, Florida, began in the late 1930s as a place to take motion pictures of marine life. Over the years it evolved into an attraction that features spectacular performing dolphins. With its original streamline moderne architecture of the 1930s enhanced by flying arches from the 1950s, the complex is now listed on the National Register of Historic Places, as is the Corn Palace in South Dakota.

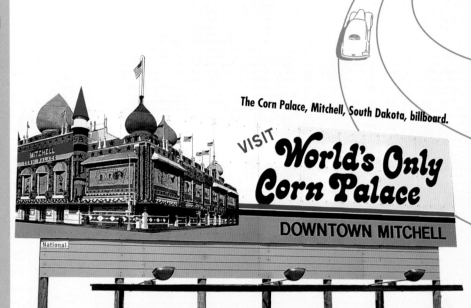

The Corn Palace, Mitchell, South Dakota, billboard.

VISIT World's Only Corn Palace

DOWNTOWN MITCHELL

Green Bay, Wisconsin.

▲ Bali-Hai Motel, Yakima, Washington.

▼ Palms Motel, Royal Oak, Michigan.

Motels

After a full day of eating short-order food, refilling gas tanks, and driving hundreds of miles, the weary traveler finally reaches the end of the road—the grand motel. In the days before Holiday Inns, the choice of where to spend the night was often based on spur-of-the-moment and sometimes irrational premises. A catchy, reassuring word or image was enough to make one stop.

Even though most motel rooms are pretty much alike, some owners have featured signage that celebrates their own specific geographical uniqueness. The Mid-Iowa motel sign reminds the sleepy driver that amidst all the cornfields, he is halfway through the state. The Bali-Hai in central Washington state evokes a vision of slumbering in a tropical paradise beneath a palm tree in Yakima. Other motel owners attempted to capitalize on the quality of the experience itself—the Kozy Kamp, the It'll Do, the Linger Longer, or the Wanda-Inn.

Motel signs project an infinite variety of small ideas to suggest positive attributes of the facilities within. Back when swimming pools were a new and exciting idea at the

PARTIAL VIEW RAMBLERS' REST — ROUTE No. 2, 1 MI.

Ramblers' Rest, Painted Post, New York, postcard circa 1940.

➤ **Top Star Motel, Aurora, Colorado.**

Komfort Court, Highway 101, King City, California.

Wanda-Inn, Carolina Beach, North Carolina.

Bellboy Motel, Wichita, Kansas.

▼ Candy Motel, Highway 99, Fresno, California.

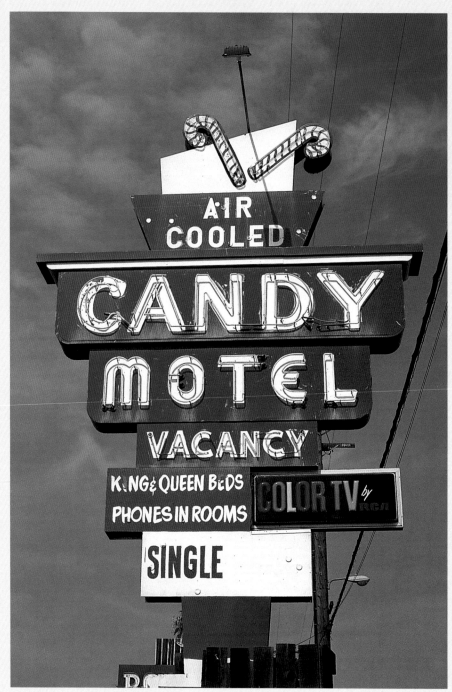

roadside, the signs showed swimmers, usually female, mid-dive, gracefully promoting a pool that was seldom used. The Lincolnville Motel, with Honest Abe's profile beaming down from above, indicated honesty, sincerity, and patriotism.

When the owner's name itself could be signified, as was done at Mr. Hammer's motel in Nebraska, personalized treatment and family pride were implied as definite benefits, even though connotations of the hammer might strike a jarring note. At the Nite Cap Motel, a nightgowned dreamer holding up a candlestick projects a more convincing image of peace and quiet.

In Colorado, one particularly elaborate sign pulls out all stops. The San-Ayre Court uses its name to describe the quality of the mountain air, a green neon shamrock to boast of the owner's Irishness, and the profile of a black scotty dog to connote either a love of Falla or a love of dogs, suggesting not too subtly that people who love dogs must be nice people.

The tepee-shaped building was a great idea for a motor court—it was both a sign and a symbol. Automotive nomads could feel right at home in these conical dwellings originally designed by Indians of the Great Plains. The biggest tepee motel chain was begun in 1936, when a man named Frank Redford noticed a tepee-shaped ice cream stand in Long Beach, California. He liked it so much that after he returned to his home in Horse Cave, Kentucky, he opened the first of a chain of seven Wigwam Village motels. Redford patented his Wigwam idea, but that didn't discourage competition, as evidenced by the Wig-Wam Courts in Texas and the Wigwam Lodge in Arizona.

With visions of neon symbols dancing in their heads, travelers might get lucky and catch a night's sleep in these "homes-away-from-home." Next morning, filled to the brim with eggs and bacon and lots of coffee, the automotive explorer would slide behind the wheel to begin again the exhilarating experience of the grand procession of American commerce—bombardment by a whole new series of intriguing and inviting signs and symbols promising everything imaginable under the sun.

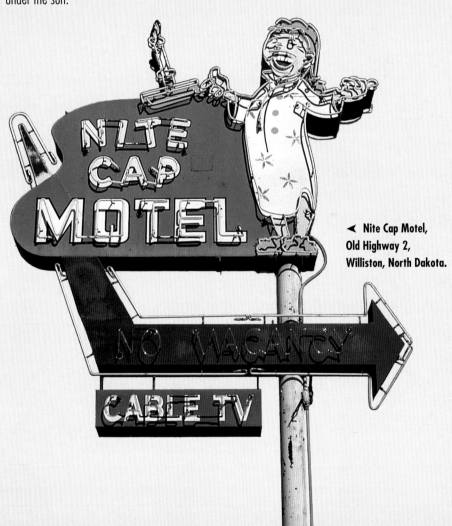

◄ Nite Cap Motel, Old Highway 2, Williston, North Dakota.

DineAville Motel & Cafe
800 West Main
VERNAL, UTAH

Motel signs project a single-minded, strong idea—STOP, exhausted, over-the-line motorist, stop, if only for a few fitful hours.

A large friendly brontosaurus holds out a sign for Motel DineAville in Vernal, Utah, even though this pink, extinct creature doesn't have much to do with a good night's sleep. It reinforces Vernal's claim to "dinosaur capital of the United States." In the nearby town of Dinosaur, Colorado, the major streets are named in honor of these long-gone beasts ("Meet you at the corner of Third and Stegosaurus").

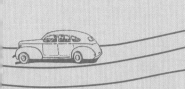

PLEASS GO 'WAY
AND LET ME SLEEP

DO NOT DISTURB

▲ Crane Motel, Roswell, New Mexico.

◄ Flamingo Motel, Oklahoma City, Oklahoma.

◄ Wigwam Village No. 2, Cave City, Kentucky.

▼ Lookout Mountain Tourist Lodge, Chattanooga, Tennessee.

▼ El Palomino Motel, Highway 6, Grand Junction, Colorado.

▼ Chief Motel, Pinellas Park, Florida.

*D*epicting Indian symbols was once a good way for motels along the paved trails of America to conjure up the spirit of "the old West." Brightly colored neon was a particularly effective means for showing off an elaborate feathered headdress. But nowadays this kind of imagery is regarded as ethnically insensitive, even though Indian, Chief, Squaw, and Teepee symbology still exists. Teepee buildings are perhaps the most common "duck" type of architecture in America. At the Wigwam Village in Kentucky, a giant teepee is a gift shop/restaurant, and the little teepees are individual tourist cabins furnished in Western style.

➤ **Chief Motel,
Montrose, Colorado.**

The bold and adventuresome cowboy bedecked in full Western attire—chaps, boots, spurs, and a ten-gallon hat—dramatizes the romance of the Old West. On Route 66 in Amarillo, a particularly resplendent cowpoke from the 1950s clashes with modern amenities such as color cable TV and waterbeds.

The saguaro symbolizes the grandeur and natural beauty of the great Southwest. Very often a sleepy Mexican, his sombrero tipped forward, is shown nodding off against the side of the prickly vegetation—an image every bit as ethnically insensitive as roadside Indians.

▼ Cowboy Motel, Route 66, Amarillo, Texas.

◄ The Wrangler Motel, Colorado Springs, Colorado.

◄ Rio Siesta Motel, Route 66, Clinton, Oklahoma.

▼ Will Rogers Motor Court, Route 66, Tulsa, Oklahoma.

◄ Cactus Inn Motel, Route 66, McLean, Texas.

United Motor Court, Redwood Highway, California, photo postcard.

M O T E L

Bear Paw
COURT
TRAILER SPACE
VACANCY

◄ Bear Paw Court, Route 2,
Chinook, Montana.

Man's best friend projects a homey, family atmosphere, the kind of place where children and pets would certainly be welcome. The Scotts ordered their Scotty's Cottages sign, outlined in vivid pink neon, from a local signmaker, who copied the design from a bakelite pin very popular in the 1940s. When the Scotts sold the business and moved away, the new owners, who were not "Scotts," destroyed the great sign. Charlene Scott would love to have had it in her new home as a memento of the family's years in the tourist cabin business.

▲ San-Ayre Court, Colorado Springs, Colorado.

➤ Audubon Court, Highway 1,
St. Augustine, Florida, postcard.

Ⅴ Scotty's Cottages,
Au Sable, Michigan.

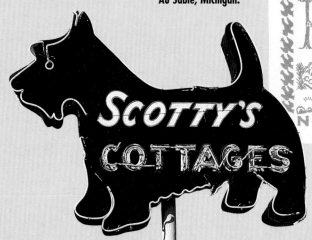

Acknowledgments

Our thanks to:

Walton Rawls, our editor, who knows a good sign when he sees one; Molly Shields, our designer, for her esthetic sensitivity; and Lewis Baer, Andreas Brown, Angela Miller, Rich Musante, Leland and Crystal Payton, Karen Shatzkin, Roger Steckler, and Tom Todd.

Those organizations and individuals who helped to sponsor and underwrite the costs of the photography: the Architectural League of New York; Tom Bailey; Susan Butler; Asher Edelman; Rosalie Genevro; The Howard Gilman Foundation; Toni Greenberg; the John Simon Guggenheim Memorial Foundation; Agnes Gund; Ellen Harris; Barbara Jakobson; Philip Johnson; the Sidney and Francis Lewis Foundation; Jim McClure; the Design Arts and Visual Arts Programs of the National Endowment for the Arts in Washington, D.C., a federal agency; the New York Foundation for the Arts; and Virginia Wright.

Photo Credits

All color photographs, 1976-1992, taken by John Margolies. Supplementary visual materials come from the authors' collections, except as noted:

Washington St., Boston, postcard, page 48, from the Roger Steckler collection; Knapp's Good Food pamphlet, page 56, from the Rich Musante collection; Sisson's Coffee Pot postcard, page 56, Largest Tiger Muskie postcard, page 61, and Halifax Creamery postcard, page 64, all from the Gotham Book Mart collection, New York City; Indiana Beach Miniature Golf postcard and Conneaut Lake Miniature Golf postcard, page 80, both from the Roger Steckler collection.

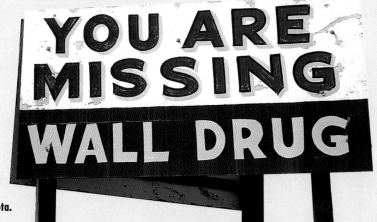

Wall Drug, Wall, South Dakota.

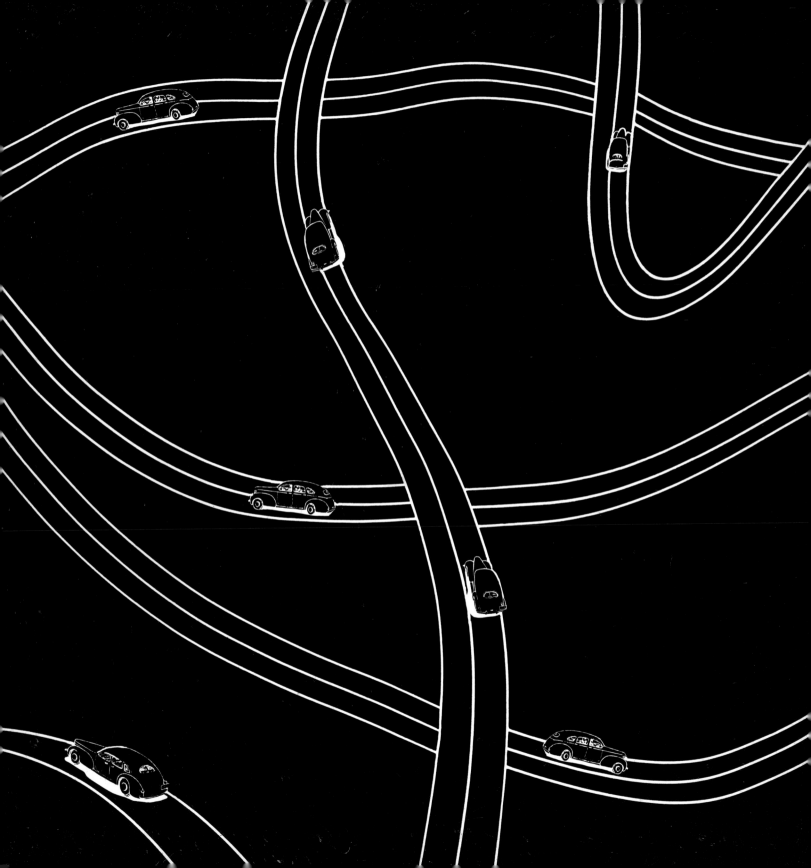